Your Aging Parents

Selected other books by Earl A. Grollman

Bereaved Children and Teens: A Support Guide for Parents and Professionals (editor)

Caring and Coping When Your Loved One Is Seriously Ill

Concerning Death: A Practical Guide for the Living (editor)

Living When a Loved One Has Died

Straight Talk About Death for Teenagers

Suicide: Prevention, Intervention, Postvention

Talking about Death: A Dialogue between Parent and Child

Talking about Divorce and Separation: A Dialogue between Parent and Child

Time Remembered: A Journal for Survivors

What Helped Me When My Loved One Died (editor)

When Someone You Love Has Alzheimer's (with Kenneth S. Kosik)

The Working Parent Dilemma (with Gerri L. Sweder)

Selected other books by Sharon Grollman

More Time to Grow: Explaining Mental Retardation to Children

Setting the Stage: Including Children with Disabilities in Head Start (with Joanne P. Brady, Peggy Enright, and Carol Howard)

Shira: A Legacy of Courage

Supporting Children with Challenging Behaviors: Relationships Are Key (with Peggy Enright and Carol Howard)

Teaching Children Affected by Substance Abuse (with Joanne P. Brady)

Your Aging Parents

Reflections for Caregivers

Earl A. Grollman
and
Sharon Grollman

Beacon Press: Boston

Beacon Press
25 Beacon Street
Boston, Massachusetts 02108-2892

Beacon Press books
are published under the auspices of
the Unitarian Universalist Association of Congregations.

03 02 01 00 99 98 97   8 7 6 5 4 3 2 1

Text design by Wesley B. Tanner/Passim Editions
Composition by Wilsted & Taylor Publishing Services

Library of Congress Cataloging-in-Publication Data
Grollman, Earl A.
    Your aging parents : reflections for caregivers /
  Earl A. Grollman and Sharon Grollman.
        p.   cm.
    Rev. ed. of: Caring for your aged parents, © 1978.
    ISBN 0-8070-2799-5 (paper)
    1. Aging parents—United States—Family relationships.
  2. Aging parents—Care—United States.   3. Aging parents—
  United States—Psychology.   4. Adult children—United States—
  Psychology.   5. Parent and child—United States.   I. Grollman,
  Sharon Hya.   II. Grollman, Earl A. Caring for your aged parents.
  III. Title.
  HQ1064.U5G72   1997
  306.874—dc21   97-11597

To my children
and grandchildren
who help me
to grow
until I go.

E.A.G.

For Dad,
who has always been there for me
while helping countless others.
Your wisdom, your humor, your love
—your life—has been a gift to us all.

S.G.

"Cast me not off in time of old age;
when my strength fails,
forsake me not."

PSALM 71:9

Contents

What This Book Is About   xi

1.   You, the Children of Aging Parents   1

2.   Your Parents   23

3.   Parents on Their Own   83

4.   Parents Living with Their Children   107

5.   Parents in a Nursing Home   123

6.   Caring and Understanding   151

For Further Help   167

Acknowledgments   173

What This Book Is About

Few changes in life are as difficult to handle as the aging of our parents. The people who fed, clothed, and protected us may now be physically weak and emotionally dependent. The reversal of roles may create stress for everyone involved.

Grown children are often unable to accept the changes without fear, resistance, and sorrow. Feelings of love and loyalty may mingle with anger and guilt. Because these emotions can be so complex and intense, it is often difficult to know what's best for our elderly parents and for ourselves. *Your Aging Parents* is written to help you better understand your own reactions as well as to meet your parents' needs.

This book includes information about a wide array of supportive community services for elderly parents still able to be independent. For those who cannot manage alone, we explore possible alternative housing arrangements, including parents living with their children, and suggest criteria for choosing a nursing home, if that proves necessary. More important, we emphasize that you and your parents can communicate more effectively and work together creatively to find solutions that work.

A note about the format: You will notice that this book looks like poetry. We are not poets, but we have used the format as a way of speaking in a direct, conversational tone and conveying useful information quickly and succinctly.

1. You, the Children of Aging Parents

"It won't happen.
   My parents won't grow old,
   need me,
   depend on me.

"Other people's parents grow old.
   Not mine."

   You remember they said:

"Don't worry about us.
   We'll never be a burden to you.
   The last thing we'd do is
   go to our children for help."

Their intentions were honest, but
the promises were unrealistic.

Your parents *do* need you.

And you are totally unprepared.

The strong and comforting people
who once nurtured you
are now in need of
your strength and comfort.

The roles have changed.

Your parents may sometimes act more like
children—

dependent,
demanding,
needing more, perhaps, than you can give,
resenting that they need
anything from you
at all.

You may find yourself reacting
in unexpected ways.

You find you still need their love,
and maybe resent that you weren't given
more of it.

Or you miss the strength
on which you once relied.

You must understand your
    disbelief,
    anger,
    guilt,
    panic,
    physical reactions,

if you are to deal successfully with your emotions.

Disbelief

"My parents haven't changed.
    (Not much, anyway.)

"So they stumble once in a while.
    (Probably need new glasses.)

"They forget to turn off the stove.
    (Everyone makes mistakes.)"

You may make all kinds of excuses.

If you don't admit what's happening to them,
then it may not be true.

It's a way of saying,

"I don't want to think about it.
Not now, anyway."

Disbelief is often a first reaction to change,
a denial of painful events,
a defense against emotional involvement.

But pretending that nothing is wrong
may prevent you from seeking and finding available help.

Anger

You are angry with yourself
for not being able to deal with
your parents without resentment.

You may be furious with your brothers or sisters

for their unreasonable suggestions,
their unjustified criticism,
lack of understanding.

Taking care of elderly parents
can create more internal strife among siblings
than the eventual reading of the will.

No matter how much you love your parents, you may feel bitter.

When you ask:
"How much do I owe them?"
You may remember:

the times they favored your brother or sister,
punished you for things
    you hadn't done;
were unkind to your spouse or friends.

"I never lived up to their expectations
   then,
What do they expect of me
   now?

      my time?
      my money?
      my life?"

You are caught in a trap:

How can you fulfill your
duty to your parents
and your responsibility for your own family
and lead your own life
and achieve your own goals?

You are frustrated or even enraged
because you feel you are
failing. You can't keep
these commitments.

Guilt

You raise your voice against your parents,

Later you resolve:

"It won't happen again."

The promise is soon forgotten.

You shout again and again.

You feel guilty.

"After all they've done for me."

You're ashamed of

    your "irrational" outbursts,
    your parents' feelings of disappointment in you,
    your embarrassment at the way they are now acting.

You're bruised by your conflicting emotions.

The more you feel you are
shortchanging your parents,
the greater your self-recrimination.

Especially if, even for a moment,
you allow yourself to think:

"It would be easier for everybody
if they died."

You are not the only one to have had
such a thought.

Panic

You are overburdened.

Your mind is in a jumble;
you can't concentrate on the tasks at hand.

If only you could run away, anywhere.

Human beings can tolerate almost
anything as long as they
have some hope that the situation will get better.

But your parents may only get worse.

You feel hopeless.

Physical Reactions

Emotional stress affects your
physical well-being.

Perhaps you experience:
    exhaustion,
    headaches,
    insomnia,
    stomach trouble,
    the need to sleep, just to escape.

Each of these symptoms may occur alone,
or in any combination
or degree of intensity.

Accepting Your Emotions

You are not alone
in your anxiety and anguish.

The resentment, shame, and irritation
are indications of the pain
you are going through.

Accepting your reactions as natural
can help you resolve them.

Finding answers for your parents
and for yourself
is a long, difficult process.

There are probably no solutions that will
satisfy everyone involved.

You can, however, choose the best one.

It will be worth the effort.

2. Your Parents

Your parents look in the mirror
and feel betrayed.

Old age is not the season of vanity.
Hair turns gray.
Skin is wrinkled.
The body is stooped.

It is as if they are ravaged
by an unseen enemy.

Physical Problems

Sometimes changes in outward appearance
are signs of physical infirmities.

Most elderly people
have one or more chronic health problems.

Most of the difficulties involve some loss
of motor or sensory abilities.

Some physical problems may be preventable.
Many can be treated and perhaps controlled.

It is essential that your parents
receive the best medical care available.

Unfortunately, older patients do not
always receive appropriate treatment.

Hospitals often favor
younger patients.

A 60-year-old and an 85-year-old
face the same grim diagnosis,
but the 85-year-old generally receives inferior treatment.

It is wrong to assume
that the elderly won't
desire or benefit from
similar medical assistance.

Many physicians are not well trained
in assisting the aging population.

Of the 684,000 medical doctors in the United States today,
only 20,000 are certified geriatricians.

Without experienced and understanding care,
the elderly may be deserted
at their most vulnerable time of life.

All discrimination is wrong,
including age discrimination.

Advocate for your parents' right
to quality medical care.

Hearing

"I don't hear as well as I used to.
  People have to shout and
  repeat things.
  I hope to God I'm not
  going deaf."

Hearing loss is the most widespread
impairment associated with aging.

Your parents may use up so much energy
concentrating on listening,
straining to hear,
that they are emotionally and physically exhausted
(and so are you).

Loss of hearing is an invisible handicap.
Other people may think they just
aren't interested
or paying attention to what is
being said.

When people can't hear clearly,
they can't make accurate judgments
or respond appropriately.

Partial deafness can cause anxiety,
maladjustment, and isolation, creating
discomfort in group situations,
where noisy conversations interfere with
understanding what's being said.

Lack of understanding can cause
suspicion and paranoia.

Loss of hearing can contribute to depression.

Suggest to your parents
that they have a complete hearing examination.

Rehabilitation programs providing the services of
    an audiologist (a nonmedical specialist trained
      in fitting hearing aids),
    a speech pathologist, and
    an otologist (ear doctor)
can determine the type of hearing loss.

Surgical intervention may be used to rectify
conductive loss when the outer ear and
middle ear are closed off
by infection or allergy.

Hearing aids are often prescribed for
sensorineural loss, which involves damage to
or malformation of the inner ear or auditory nerves.

Although parents rarely need to be persuaded
to use eyeglasses and dentures,
they often rebel against wearing hearing aids.

Try to convince them that pride
should not prevent their getting
sorely needed assistance.

It will help for them to admit
that they just don't hear well,
and to say:

"I'm sorry,
I didn't hear you.
Will you say it again?"

There are other ways to
minimalize the problem of hearing loss:

    a flashing lamp to replace a fire alarm system;

    inexpensive television attachments that increase
        the sound without disturbing other listeners;

    an adjustable wheel on the handset of the telephone,
    which amplifies the voice of the person on the
        other end;

    a flashing light instead
        of a bell on the telephone
            or doorbell.

When you talk to your hard-of-hearing parents:

Speak face-to-face in a well-lighted area, and
keep your hands away from your face.
Seeing your expressions will help them
interpret your words.

Speak in a normal fashion without shouting or
elaborately mouthing words.

Recognize that people don't hear so well
when they are tired or sick.

Dull ears don't mean a dull mind.

Vision

"For quite a while I pretended that
   I was tired.
   The lighting was poor.
   But it's my eyes.
   I just don't see well anymore."

Vision changes with age.

The muscles that control pupil dilation
to help our eyes adjust to light
are altered.

There is a higher incidence of
glaucoma (increased pressure) and
cataracts (clouding of the lens).

Visual or hearing loss may discourage parents
from joining in social activities.
These impairments may curtail or eliminate such pastimes as
reading, watching television, or doing handiwork,
and interfere with mobility and orientation.

Sometimes elders are labeled "senile"
when their only problem
is poor vision.

A thorough eye examination can
determine whether stronger eyeglasses
or corrective surgery
is necessary.

Visual aids are readily available:

Large-print books, magazines, newspapers.

Talking-book machines and computers,
recording services.

Low-vision aids, from simple magnifying glasses
to telescopic eyeglasses.

Sophisticated machinery that translates
print to raised letters
or to spoken words.

They may need more time than usual
to prepare to go out of the house.

Maybe you are taking them to the doctor.

They have their hats and coats on an hour before
the appointment, even though you've assured them
that the trip to the office will take fifteen minutes.

They call, "Why aren't you ready?"

It's their way of expressing anxiety about the visit,
about what they may learn from the doctor.

But they also need more time to walk to the car, to the elevator.

Understand their slower movement
and their need to adjust to it.

Some conditions require
a cane or walker for support,
or even a wheelchair.
But remember that a person in a wheelchair
sees the world differently
from those standing upright.

The person has to look up to see.

Muscles are cramped.

Make sure that you always
tell your parent where and when
you are pushing the wheelchair.
Don't jolt their nerves and bodies.

Lock the wheelchair
when it is in place.

Rehabilitation centers can provide your parents
with physical and occupational therapy
to improve their mobility and
increase their self-reliance.

Assessment by home care agencies
can offer suggestions
for making your parents' home
a safer environment.

Taste

"I'm not hungry.
  Besides, the food tastes flat.
  More salt, please."

Because older people's sense of taste
is less acute,
they often demand more highly
seasoned foods.

But this can be dangerous if they are on a
low-sodium or salt-free diet.

A nutritionist can help to plan
wholesome and palatable diets.

Sensation of Pain, Heat, Cold

Aging often causes a sharp decrease in the ability
to identify sensations of pain.

Older people, aware of discomfort,
are often unable to isolate its source.
Something as localized as an ingrown toenail,
infected tooth, impacted bowel,
may not be recognized as such.

The frustration of feeling miserable
and not knowing the cause
may lead to irritability.

With age, thermal senses also become impaired.

Unaware of the temperature of the bath water,
older people may scald themselves.

On the other hand, they are more sensitive
to cold weather.

While everyone else is sweltering,
they grumble that the heat should be
turned up.

An extra sweater or blanket
might be all that's needed.

Sexuality

"Sexual joy is reserved for the young,
  for those in the first decades of life."

"The elderly have no need for
  sexual satisfaction."

"Especially after years of living alone,
  they are sexually impotent."

These statements are false and misleading.

Society has misunderstood the
sexual interests of older people.

Sex life for the elderly is not inappropriate,
nor are those who have sex
"dirty old men (or women)."

Physical affection—holding, hugging, closeness—
is as necessary and comforting
for the old as for the young.

The elderly have the right to live
and to love as fully as they are able.

Memory

"I keep forgetting things.
  Important dates.
  Appointments.
  Doctor's instructions.
  Whether I turned off the stove.
  Where I left my glasses.
  People's names—my closest friends."

"I feel as if I'm losing my mind."

  Most older people experience
  these changes to some degree.

  What happened yesterday and today is hazy,
  uncertain, sometimes completely forgotten.

  Yet they recall past events with great accuracy.

There are many reasons
for memory problems:

  arteriosclerosis—the hardening and narrowing
      of the arteries,
  side effects of medication,
  malnutrition,
  disorientation because of a new situation
      or new surroundings,
  depression and anxiety,
  an illness, like dementia or Alzheimer's disease.

To get to the root of the problem,
consult a physician.

Do not accept glib answers, like
"What can you expect at that age?"
    or
"A little confusion is normal
    for this time of life."

A psychiatric evaluation
in conjunction with neurological tests
may help the doctor determine what the problem is.

Very often, the problem may be treatable
if it is identified early.

Do not accept
"It's the aging process"
    for any physical or mental change
    without ruling out other possibilities first.

Your greatest fear may be Alzheimer's disease,
the progressive brain disorder,
fatal but slow,
lingering through years of decline and dependency.

Know that your parent's forgetfulness
is not necessarily a symptom of Alzheimer's.
Having difficulty remembering names and events
is almost universal among elders.

Experts call this normal process
"age-associated memory loss."

Testing for Alzheimer's disease
requires but a few blood tests,
often a brain scan, and
sometimes a neuropsychological evaluation
to measure problem-solving ability,
memory, and the use of language.

Evaluation is not painful or time consuming.

The examination can help to allay your fears.

A mind paralyzed by terror
is not dissimilar
to one wiped clean by Alzheimer's.

If your parent has Alzheimer's disease,
you might fear that you are fated
to inherit the same disease.

While some forms of Alzheimer's run in families,
it is extremely rare.

Even among identical twins,
one may have the disease
and the other, not.

For all kinds of memory loss,
you can help your parents' memories by:

> associating a name with some event or person
> > ("You remember, Connie brought you the cheesecake"),
> repeating unfamiliar names often
> > ("Your new neighbors, the Kearns"),
> writing down the physician's instructions immediately
> > ("The doctor said two pills four times a day"),
> using a large, clear calendar to make their appointments.

An occasional telephone call helps to reinforce matters
that shouldn't be forgotten or overlooked,
and it reminds your parents that you care.

Reassure them that
we *all* need help to remember.

Losses

In addition to physical changes,
age brings
psychological losses too.

Old age has been referred to as
"the season of losses."

For good reason.

Personal Losses

Your parents have a diminishing circle
of people who are important to them.

Death robs them of
siblings,
other relatives,
colleagues,
friends,
a spouse,
even—sometimes—their children.

Social and Financial Losses

The compensations of work are gone.

Not just the money,
but the self-esteem and satisfactions
that formed the structure
of their earlier years.

More time is spent at home.

Mother and father may get on each other's nerves.

Perhaps reluctant to participate in
outside social and recreational activities,
they create a self-imposed isolation.

They see themselves as being in the way,
on the fringes of life.

The Vicious Circle

In the aging process
one loss can lead to another:

> decline of physical health,
> decreased activity,
> lowered earning capacity,
> loss of independence,
> changes in relationships with family and friends,
> physical and social isolation,
> low self-esteem,
> depression,
> mental illness.

Old age can indeed be a losing game.

Mental Illness

"I sometimes wonder in the morning
  if life is worth getting up for."

The pressures on your parents
—physical, emotional, social, and personal—
may be unbearable.

So many painful situations arise
just when they are least able
to cope with them.

And because mental impairment is regarded
as inevitable and irreversible in old people,
they rarely get the help they need.

Remembering brings a sharp pain.

"Most everyone I know is gone."

Your parents may be

apathetic,
ready to argue at the slightest excuse,
suspicious of everyone—including you,
complaining continually,
confused, disoriented,
reacting with exaggerated emotional outbursts
    that are out of proportion to the causes,
unconcerned about personal hygiene,
unable to experience pleasure.

Parents' emotional changes often evoke
feelings of anxiety and hostility
in their children.

You may express these feelings by saying,
"Snap out of it!"

It doesn't do any good.

Your irritation demonstrates an inability
to handle the stressful situation,
and pushes you and your parents
farther apart.

"All I have left is death."

Self-destruction may be
their solution to a life without hope.

Some warning signals may be

Physical attempt
Twelve percent of those who attempt suicide
will try again and will succeed within two years.

Verbal threat
Those who do take their lives
often speak about it beforehand.

Slow suicide
Death-oriented behavior includes
    self-starvation,
    refusal to follow doctor's prescriptions and orders,
    hazardous activity,
    voluntary seclusion.

For professional help contact:

The family physician
A starting point for medical help and for
referrals to specialists and treatment resources.

A geriatrician
Who specializes in
helping the elderly.

A psychiatrist
For an assessment of emotional problems.

Mental health agencies
Licensed social workers, clinical psychologists,
and family counselors.

A family conference,
perhaps with a psychiatric social worker as mediator, might help
you understand your role
in assisting your parents.

Many psychological services are fully or partially funded
by personal insurance policies, Medicare, or Medicaid.

Medication

Medication therapy can often combat
depression, the consequences of arteriosclerosis,
and slowed body and muscle movement.

Medication use can also become drug abuse
when the elderly are confused about
the proper directions to follow
or when they hoard old bottles.

Help them by checking their medicine cabinet.
Remove unmarked prescriptions and old medicines.

Have them keep a card containing
a list of their medications, including

dosage and frequency,
reason for taking,
prescribing physician,
and names and phone numbers of doctors and relatives.

Have your parent ask the doctor
the purpose of the medication,
how long before the drug takes effect,
possible side effects, such as dry mouth,
    loss of appetite, drowsiness, nausea,
long-term consequences,
addictive possibilities.

Written instructions are especially helpful.

Inform the physician of other medicines
your parents are taking.
A chemical stew could trigger
unexpected and dangerous reactions.

Antacids for an ulcer can inhibit the effect of an
antibiotic being taken to cure an infection.

Such foods as fruit juices and milk
may reduce the effectiveness of some medicines.

Alcohol combined with sedatives can be lethal.

Every drug has a potential for
harm as well as for therapeutic relief.

If you notice unusual side effects,
inform the doctor immediately.

Informed Consent

"Why should my parents
  know what's wrong with them?
  It would kill them.
  They could never handle it."

If you don't share medical information with your parents,
you may be sparing yourself,
but not them.

They'll be able to sense
your fears
by your discomfort, defensiveness, and flight.

When parents are aware of their problems,
they can participate in necessary decisions.

If they learn the truth later,
they may resent their doctor and
lose confidence in you.

The most troubling reality is
often easier to accept
than uncertainty.

Dying and Death

Each experience with illness,
each realization that another faculty is impaired
may arouse your parents' conscious and
unconscious anxieties about dying.

They may think a great deal about
how much time they have to live.

Parents' worst nightmares may not even be of death,
but of a long-term illness that

> wipes out their financial resources,
> makes them totally dependent on others,
> condemns them to unending, excruciating pain,
> suspends them indefinitely between life and death.

Dying, the natural conclusion of the life cycle,
has been mercifully delayed by medical
and public health measures.

Revolutionary technological advances make it
possible to prolong the
lives of those older patients
who previously would not have survived.

But the good news is punctuated by the bad.
Unfortunately, as the population lives longer,
Many die more slowly—and in pain.

It has been estimated that some
terminal patients—perhaps five percent—
die in intractable pain.

Some are hooked up to breathing
machines and feeding tubes—
in agony,
living a fate worse than death.

If your parents are dying,
you might consider hospice care.
Hospice neither hastens nor postpones death.

It stresses care and support, not cure.

Even though hospice care
is less expensive and more palliative,
most patients enter too late to receive
maximum benefits.

It is estimated that the average
patient enters only thirty-six days before dying,
fifteen percent one week before death.

A pity: Too little psychological, medical, and spiritual help
can be rendered during these last few days.

Your aging parents need health-care professionals
who will communicate effectively,
ensuring that medical treatment
promotes physical and emotional well-being,
encouraging the highest possible quality of life,
controlling pain and respecting your parents'
needs and wishes.

It takes wisdom and tenderness
to distinguish quality care
from procedures
that needlessly prolong suffering.

Before it's too late,
encourage your parents to decide if they would want

cardiac resuscitation,
mechanical respiration,
antibiotics,
tube feeding

in the event of

terminal treatment,
coma,
irreversible brain damage.

They may choose to minimize pain,
even when it may hasten death.

There are advance directives (see For Further Help, End-of-Life
        Decisions, p. 168)
a broad term for "living will"
and the durable power of attorney.

All states and the District of Columbia, with variations,
recognize the legality of the document.

How wise and courageous it is
when a parent of free will and sound mind
can express these critically important decisions
with family, clergy, attorney, and physicians.

Often the elderly accept the certainty of death more willingly than the young do.

You may be uncomfortable knowing
that your parents will someday die.

It forces you to realize that
you, too, are growing old.

Suddenly, you begin to confront
your own mortality.

3. Parents on Their Own

Perhaps you now have a clearer understanding
of your parents' losses—
both physical and emotional.

Remember, however, that an impairment
need not imply a disengagement from life.

Your parents may still be able to
live with purpose and meaning.

By changing the supports in their environment,
you can help them maintain as much
independence as possible.

Those who make the best adjustment to old age
are those who have outside interests,
pleasant social relations with friends and relatives,
and a role in society.

And, most important,
their own space
with privacy and independence.

Having their own space affords
them a sense of

Autonomy
the ability to live their lives
in their own way.

Intimacy
the familiar scene, providing
continuity and security.

Identity
the sense of pride and satisfaction
in maintaining a sense of individuality.

But your parents may not be able to
take care of themselves completely.

You may be concerned about their
    medical needs,
    nutrition,
    personal hygiene, and
    emotional well-being.

Is a nursing home the only solution?
What are the alternatives?

Community Resources

An institution is not the only answer
for parents with special needs.

Community-sponsored and
private organizations offer
various kinds of help for
elderly people who want to remain in their homes.

Consult your local Council on Aging
for information about
these and other services
available in your community.

Visiting Nurses

If your parents are
suffering from a chronic illness,
recovering from sickness, or
in need of bedside care,
you might contact a visiting nurse association.

Nurses will come regularly
to provide your parents with
medication and injections,
wound and bandage care,
blood pressure checks, and
physical therapy.

Nurses' visits
can shorten hospitalization
by filling vital medical needs
in familiar surroundings.

Visiting nurses can also provide
respite care for caregivers.

For any services, check in advance
to determine who will pay, and for
how long.

Home Health Aides

A trained person, working under
the supervision of a nurse, social worker,
or other professional,
assists your parents in

Homemaker services
food shopping, personal errands, light housekeeping.

Hygienic duties
giving baths, changing dressings,
helping with prescribed exercises.

Information and referral services
providing emotional support in times of stress,
with referral to appropriate resources.

Home-Delivered Meals

Some programs prepare
nutritious meals, which are delivered
directly to the homes of the elderly,
with perhaps a sandwich, fruit, and dessert
to be refrigerated for later in the day.

Social interaction
with concerned volunteers
is an added benefit.

Make sure the food
fits your parents'
therapeutic diet.

Telephone Reassurance Program

Especially if your parents live far away,
you can arrange for
volunteers to call your parents
at convenient times.

The caller
checks on the well-being of your parents, and
helps to mitigate their loneliness and to
relieve their fears.

Since you know that the call will be made,
you can be less anxious about your parents falling,
or becoming ill, and being unable to call for help.

You know that emergency aid would be forthcoming.

A key holder should be
prearranged in the
event that no one responds to the call.

Homemaker Services

Homemakers provide

Housekeeping
assisting in laundry, cleaning,
meal preparation, and errands.

Yard and walk maintenance
snow removal and lawn cutting.

This service is recommended for those
capable of caring for themselves
but needing help in and around their homes.

Some homemaker services also provide assistance in
daily living, including
eating, dressing, and bathing.

Transportation and Escort Services

Some communities provide transportation for seniors
who need personal assistance to go to the
doctor, shopping center, bank, library, or
senior citizens' center when

public transportation is unavailable
or inaccessible, or parking is not
close to the destination.

seniors cannot board and travel on
buses, subways, trains, or need special help to do so.

an escort is needed to secure a service and
ensure a safe return home.

Friendly Visitors Program

Volunteers visit your parents on a
regularly scheduled basis,
filling leisure hours with
card playing, letter writing, and
reading aloud.

The visitors will listen sympathetically
and try to help your parents
make their own decisions,
develop new interests,
revive old hobbies,
and strengthen their links with the outside community.

Senior Social Centers

Senior Social Centers give your parents
an opportunity
to leave the isolation of their home
and enjoy recreation with others.

Many centers offer:

Group programs
classes in bridge, yoga, indoor gardening,
    arts and crafts.

Cultural recreation
concerts, theater, field trips, visits to
    historic sites.

Nutrition
hot lunches, classes in proper food planning.

Counseling and referral.
psychological help, crisis intervention,
    referral to appropriate agencies,
    and information about
    government and private entitlement programs.

Geriatric Day Programs and Hospitals

These centers are designed for older people who
have a combination of physical, mental, and social
limitations, but do not need to be institutionalized.

Instead, they spend the day in a clinic, nursing home, or
hospital-based facility where
occupational and physical therapy, therapeutic recreation,
psychotherapy, and medical services
are available.

Physical and psychological programs help
the elderly to remain functioning members
in their communities,
reducing family tension for their children
who are busy during the day.

To find out about other
services and programs available
in your community, such as
    respite care,
    congregate housing,
    adult foster care,
    elder housing, and
    continuing care communities,
consult your local Council on Aging.

Options and Opportunities

Efforts have been made
for the elderly who need additional support.

But little labor has been devoted
to those who are healthy,
to keep them that way
as long as possible,
and to enhance the quality of their lives.

Work

*"The sudden cessation of productive work and
earning power often leads to physical and
emotional deterioration and premature death."*
AMERICAN MEDICAL ASSOCIATION

Retirement for many is not a reward.
It can be a painful time
with little direction and few goals.

If your parents have
the desire and ability to work,
they may be able to reenter
the workforce, regaining
financial security and personal fulfillment.

They may find a place in their old profession,
or develop an interest or hobby
that could blossom into a lucrative pursuit.

Knowledge, experience, and skills
do not disappear at age sixty-five.

Volunteering

Volunteering is an opportunity to
put one's skills to use,
learn new skills,
and come into contact with new people, ideas,
and challenges.

Volunteer opportunities exist in
schools,
hospitals,
day care centers, libraries, social service organizations,
religious and fraternal organizations,
senior citizens' clubs, and
homemaker services.

Many local newspapers have special sections
that describe volunteer opportunities and
activities in their communities.

The government also sponsors both volunteer
and employment programs.

Education

Some colleges, aware of the educational
and cultural needs of older adults,
offer courses at little or no tuition cost.

Schools may bring your parents
intellectual involvement,
cultural stimulation,
and a sense of purpose.

Contact the nearest university or
adult education center in your area.

Creative Use of Leisure Time

Some people look forward
to their later years with optimism.

Old age can be both an end and a beginning:

an end to job demands, clocks, schedules.

a beginning for those things they always wanted to do
but had no time for.

Help your parents take inventory,
reflect on their disappointments and achievements,
define their present needs and future goals,
and explore those activities that bring them
the greatest enjoyment.

4. Parents Living with Their Children

If one of your parents dies,
or becomes seriously ill
and requires long-term hospital care,
you may say to the other:

"You can't manage alone.
 The house is too big for you.
 Come live with us."

You may even consider saying this to both of them,
if you're afraid they can no longer manage on their own.

Wait!

Your intentions are good.

But your actions
may not necessarily be in the best interests of
your parents,
your spouse and children,

you.

Consider your parents' needs . . .

Do they *want* to live with you, or other relatives, and
give up part of their independence?

Will they be isolated in your home,
without the security of friends, organizations,
and familiar landmarks?

Is your house large enough
to give them and you needed privacy?

There are important factors to be weighed.

Consider your family's needs . . .

What kind of relationship does the family
have with your parents?

If you and your spouse work during the day,
can your parents manage alone in your house?

Are you willing or financially able
to obtain outside help?

A three-generation household is a big
responsibility for *every* member.

If your spouse doesn't agree willingly,
the arrangement probably won't work.

And you . . .

How do you feel?

Examine your past relationship with your parents.

Themes played before in your family's history
may be repeated.

If guilt is your only motivation,
you will soon resent your parents
for intruding into your home.

Decisions must be predicated on more
than momentary guilt.

Encourage other members of your immediate family
to share their feelings about the move.

You have a better possibility of
working out the arrangements satisfactorily
when *everyone* expresses honest emotions.

If you are not an only child
don't be afraid or ashamed
to ask siblings for assistance.

Of course, your parents must be included in the decision making.

Discuss frankly what you might expect of each other
in terms of
food preparation,
chores around the house,
finances.

When your friends come to visit,
are your parents to be included in the gathering?

Will your parents feel deserted
if you and your spouse want to go out alone?

Explain your needs.
Listen to theirs.

There must be mutual understanding.

Perhaps a trial period could be arranged
to work out such details as:

Money
If they want to contribute,
instead of paying rent,
they might place funds
in a special account for your children's education.

Meals
When they don't enjoy the food you're planning
to serve, perhaps that is a good time
for them to go out with a friend.

Transportation
Be willing to take your parents to homes of friends,
the community center, or the doctor's office.

Your parents might retain their old house or apartment
during the experimental period,

just in case.

If they are able, and willing,
allow them to share household responsibilities:

    washing dishes,
    cooking,
    cleaning,
    repair work.

Asking them for help
may make them feel needed,

not like boarders.

Of course, your parents should have
their own room—a place in the house
to pursue their own interests,
without disturbing other family members
or being disturbed themselves.

Remember, they are not
your servants or babysitters.

Encourage them to
invite their friends into your home,
and to participate in activities outside the home.

There may be times when you feel
angry, cheated, violated
because of simple things like
a newspaper not returned to you intact,
the water faucet that is not turned off in the bathroom.
Even the sight of dentures may make you feel squeamish.

Or bigger issues, like
your spouse's resentment of the new responsibilities,
your children's unhappiness with the "other parents"
   who advise and criticize,
your being treated like a child by the parents
   you have to take care of.

Allow

Ample time
to determine whether the accommodation
can be successful.

Open communication
for everyone to understand the issues involved.

*"If there is separation of old
people from family life,
there is tragedy for both
young and old."*
MARGARET MEAD

5. Parents in a Nursing Home

"If my parents stay in my house
  for one more day
  I think I'll have a nervous breakdown.

But they can't manage alone."

Is a nursing home the only solution?

It depends.

Before making any decisions
examine the situation.

Are your parents
mentally alert,
able to care for their personal needs (shopping,
    food preparation, dressing),
ambulatory?

Again,
there may be community resources
available to help them remain in their homes.

Check alternatives.

Homes for the elderly, apartments in sheltered housing, assisted
      living,
retirement homes, and congregate
housing offer such diverse services as

   the serving of an evening meal,
   registered nurses or a resident physician, and
   recreational and cultural programs.

Your parents may prefer to live in these facilities,
with a degree of self-sufficiency,
under the watchful eye of concerned people.

Contact your local housing authority,
community development agency, or office on aging,
and their physician.

If community services are insufficient,
alternative housing inappropriate,
or your parents'
medical care needs too great,

a nursing home may be the only choice.

A nursing home?

"Oh, my God,
How can I do this to them?"

The decision to institutionalize
a loved one
is among the most difficult
anyone is ever required to make.

You may feel panic-stricken.

In desperation you think
you must make a decision.
Any decision would be an improvement
over the uncertainty.

But this is a time for exercising judgment,
not for a rash decision you may regret later.

If you have brothers and sisters,
do not act alone or
you may be blamed for poor judgment and
lack of consideration.

Discuss the situation with them.
While such discussions may be difficult,
your siblings' involvement may help you make better choices
for the present and the future.

Your siblings may suggest other alternatives
and even offer some financial assistance.

Your parents' participation and preparation
   are essential.

Talk *with* them,
not *at* them.

Don't tell them
what you have already decided.

Wait for those moments
when you are all rested, alert,
and able to share in the discussion.
Timing is critical.

Your tone should be gentle, conversational,
not demanding and argumentative.

You may have to explain the situation
again and again,
so that they can understand
the possible changes in their lives.

Perhaps their doctor can explain
that this is a medical decision,
not a family rejection.

Be prepared
if your parents say:

"What are you doing to me?
  A nursing home?
  So you can wash your hands of me?
  After all I've done for you!

"You promised
  you'd never put me in one of those places."

They may regard the nursing home as
the last stop,
a kind of purgatory,
halfway between society and the cemetery.

They may blame you for
the irreversible deterioration of their bodies,
their inability to take care of themselves,
your seeming unwillingness to care for their needs.

Institutionalization may seem to them
tantamount to rejection.

Tell them that
you want to understand their frustration and anxiety;
you know how hard it is for them to move
    at this stage of their lives.

Assure them that you're not hurrying;
that no decisions will be made immediately
and there will be time for them to change
    their minds.
You are merely preparing for what may be necessary.

Remind them that not all nursing homes
are cold and impersonal;
and some nursing home patients
with rehabilitation can return home.

You will need to learn about
your parents' financial situation,
and to obtain legal advice
to discern what aid you may be eligible to receive,
and whether your parents' assets can be protected.

The family attorney and accountant
could help evaluate
your parents' economic resources
by preparing an inventory of such assets as
    savings and checking accounts,
    real estate,
    pensions,
    fraternal or professional society benefits,
    insurance policies,
    trust agreements,
    veterans' benefits,
    Social Security.

Keep an account of all records
so that you can avert any family problems
in the future.

The government can help with:

Medicare
A health insurance program that pays for a
portion of hospital care as well as for
skilled nursing facilities.
Included may be physician and health services,
therapy, medical supplies.
>Contact your local Social Security office
>for details.

Medicaid
For those in low-income brackets,
payments are made for physicians and
medical services, intermediate care facilities,
and skilled nursing facilities.
>Contact your local welfare department
>to see if your parents qualify.

Supplemental Security Income (SSI)
A federal program for those in need of
financial assistance, and for people who
are blind and disabled, with automatic Medicaid coverage.
>Contact your local Social Security office
>for information.

To learn about suitable nursing homes,
ask for recommendations from
    doctors,
    social workers,
    staff from geriatric management agencies,
    clergy,
    local or state health and aging departments,
    hospital or nursing home associations,
    senior citizens' groups,
    Social Security office,
    relatives,
    friends.

Your doctor may help you match
your parents' needs
to the appropriate level of nursing home care.

While the federal government makes no
distinction in levels of care,
the following classifications may be helpful.

> *Skilled Nursing Facility (SNF)*
> twenty-four-hour nursing service
> for "convalescent" patients
> who require constant medical supervision.

> *Intermediate Care Facility (ICF)*
> less intensive medical care than that
> offered by SNFs, with a greater emphasis
> on social and rehabilitative services.

Some institutions offer both levels of care.

Before visiting a nursing home
you should call to
determine the level of care provided,
the financial arrangements, including
    Medicare and Medicaid,
and space availability.

Be sure that the home and administrator
are licensed by the state.

You may be shocked
when you first walk into a nursing home.

Many people are in wheelchairs,
or use walkers.

Some seem disoriented,
feeble.

Your reaction may be,

"My parents don't belong here."

Don't dismiss a particular home because of
your first impression.

Look further.
See if some of the residents are alert,
communicating freely with staff
and one another.

If possible, come with your parents on several occasions.
Visit unexpectedly at mealtime
and during the activities period.

Notice whether

> the atmosphere is warm and friendly;
>
> the rooms are soundproof, properly heated, air-conditioned;
>
> the area is likely to please your parents and is located conveniently near family, friends, and hospital;
>
> medical professionals are in residence or on call;
>
> there are physical, speech, and occupational therapy services, individual and group recreational activities, religious services, chaplain, beauty shop, barber;
>
> the food being served is both nutritious and flavorful;
>
> the people look relatively contented, and not drugged (women wearing makeup and men neatly dressed are good signs);
>
> the bathrooms are clean and conveniently located.

Remember, no type of facility
can serve all people effectively.
You are looking for the one
best suited to *your* parents.

Interview the administrator,
head nurse, and social worker.
Do they visit the residents regularly,
know their names?
What is the proportion of trained
professionals and volunteers to residents?

Ask the relatives of the residents
for their opinions.

Talk to the residents themselves.

Don't depend on a single source
or be unduly influenced by
an administrator's bias,
a child's guilt, or
a parent's resentment.

Careful scrutiny of the facility, patients,
and staff is an important factor in making the proper choice.

Your parents should visit
before their formal admittance
to become familiar with the
surroundings, residents, and staff.

Ease their transition by being
with them on admission day and
staying for a few hours until
they're settled.

After your parents become acclimated,
your phone calls, letters,
visits will bring them comfort and reassurance.

Occasionally, if possible, you might take them to a
restaurant or movie, and
to your home for birthdays, holidays, or
just casual visits.

As nearly as possible,
provide them with the kind of love
that you would give them
if they were at home.

Entering a nursing home is
a time of major stress for your parents.

Don't ignore this fact,
or, on the other hand, underestimate
your parents' resilience in making
a satisfactory adjustment.

Moving to a new environment
may markedly improve their morale.

6. Caring and Understanding

We feel different about life at seventy-five
than at forty-five.
Viewpoints change.

Interaction among family members
of varying ages can cause friction.

You might put aside your feelings for the moment,
and really try looking at your parents' situation
through their eyes.

Ask yourself, "How do *they* feel?"

Listening

If your parents feel that the whole world
is against them,
it is good for them to know that
some people are on their side.

You can demonstrate your concern and support
by listening to them,
especially if they have little contact
with others.

They need someone to talk to,
someone with whom they can safely share
feelings and thoughts.

Let them talk
without interruption,
even if they go off on tangents.
It is one way for them
to get things off their chests.

However, be on guard against making them
speak about those matters
that are embarrassing and
distressing to them.

If possible, encourage
friends, associates, and family to call,
write, or visit
to help them feel
part of their community.

Don't gloss over their
complaints and worries with
cheerful clichés and
patronizing reassurances,
such as:

"I only hope I'm as healthy
as you when I'm your age.
Look, your friends are worse off
than you."

Pain is pain,
anxiety is anxiety,
whatever the age of the person who feels it
and no matter how unfortunate others may be.

Sharing

As important as listening is,
so is sharing your world with them.

Talk about your personal life,
news of the family,
and events in the community.

When you seek their advice,
they know that you value their judgment.

If they can help you with your problems,
they feel like parents again,
like people with something useful
to offer others.

Acknowledging

Have you ever noticed
that you sometimes make decisions for your parents,
such as ordering their meals at a restaurant
without asking their preference, or
in the doctor's office,
answering questions concerning *their* health?

Treating older parents like helpless individuals
can be psychologically devastating to them,
undermining their self-regard and self-confidence.

They want to be treated as
subjects, not objects.

"A Soft Answer Turneth Away Wrath"

"I want to eat *now*."

You answer, "Can't you see I'm busy?"

"NOW. This minute."

You argue, but to no avail.

They still want their food NOW.

Ask yourself what you are gaining.

After the ranting and raving,
your parents may still not
understand the situation.

Sometimes it is better to submit,
and take a few moments to
give them what they want
and thus avoid conflict.

In many cases, troubled people
cannot always help what they are doing,
can't stop doing it
even when they are asked.

It may be futile to argue.

When you shout to make your point,
it is you who have lost control.

Try as gently as possible to decide
what you reasonably can and cannot expect of each other.

Laughing

A sense of humor is helpful
in times of stress.

The ability to laugh
when you're having trouble
is like bringing fresh flowers into the house
after winter has withered the garden.

Laughing at yourself
can encourage others to laugh
at themselves, too.

Approving

What person is immune to praise?

When parents' feelings are low,
your respect and admiration can raise them.

"Mom, Dad, I'm proud of you."

Notice what happens.

Praise reassures them
that they are still valued.

Touching

Touching is the most comforting
way of communicating,
a testimony to the
quality of your feelings.

When words have been exhausted,
try holding your parents' hands
or embracing them.

Celebrating

How about a party after an operation or illness?

It honors their courage.

It tells others they are alive and
could use a little notice.

It affirms that you're glad
you still have them.

Listening, sharing, touching, laughing, celebrating
creates a loving atmosphere for
your parents and
for you.

As you meet their needs,
your own needs may be met.

As you give them your hands,
you may find your own heart.

As you help them end their day,
you may find new beginnings in yourself.

For Further Help

Consult your local Council on Aging for services available in your community.

Advocacy

Gray Panthers

2025 Pennsylvania Avenue, N.W., Washington, DC 20009
202-466-3132

Canadian Grey Panthers

5225 Orbitor Drive, Unit 20, Mississauga, Ontario, Canada L4W 4Y8
905-624-1616
http://www.panthers.net

Alzheimer's

Alzheimer's Association

919 Michigan Avenue, Suite 1000, Chicago, IL 60611
800-272-3900
http://www.alz.org

Alzheimer's Disease Education and Referral Center (ADEAR)

P.O. Box 8250, Silver Spring, MD 20907
800-438-4380
http://www.alzheimers.org/adear

Caregiver Support

Children of Aging Parents

Suite 302A, 1609 Woodbourne Road, Levittown, PA 19057
800-227-7294

Manitoba Association on Gerontology

Box 1833, Winnipeg, Manitoba, Canada R3C 3R1
204-783-8389

National Family Caregivers Association

9621 East Bexhill Drive, Kensington, MD 20895
301-942-6430

End-of-Life Decisions

Choice in Dying, Inc.

200 Varick Street, New York, NY 10014
800-989-WILL

The Center to Improve Care of the Dying

George Washington Medical School
1001 22nd Street N.W., Suite 700, Washington, DC 20037
202-476-2271

Education

American Association for Adult and Continuing Education

1200 19th Street, N.W., Suite 300, Washington, DC 20036
202-429-5131

Elderhostel

75 Federal Street, 3rd Floor, Boston, MA 02110
617-426-8056
http://www.elderhostel.org

Elderhostel Canada

308 Wellington Street, Kingston, Ontario, Canada K7K 7A7
613-530-2222

Emotional/Psychological Help

Family Service Association of America

11700 West Lake Park Drive, Milwaukee, WI 53224
    414-359-1040

Hearing/Speech

National Association for Hearing and Speech Action

10801 Rockville Pike, Rockville, MD 20852
    301-897-8682

Canadian Hearing Society Foundation

330 Bay Street, Suite 1402, Toronto, Ontario, Canada M5H 2S8
    416-364-4060

Homemaker Services

Eldercare Locator, U.S. Department of Health and Human
        Services

National Association of Area Agencies on Aging
1112 16th Street, N.W., Suite 100, Washington, DC 20030
    800-667-1116

National Meals on Wheels Foundation

2675 44th Street, S.W., #305, Grand Rapids, MI 49509
    800-999-6262

Support Services to Seniors

Manitoba Health Coordinator
2nd Floor, 800 Portage Avenue, Winnipeg, Canada R3G 0N4
    204-945-8731
    or contact the Services to Seniors specialist in your area.

Nutrition

American Dietetic Association

216 West Jackson Boulevard, Chicago, IL 60609
    312-899-0040, ext. 5000
    http://www.eatright.org

Vision

National Federation of the Blind

1800 Johnson Street, Baltimore, MD 21230
    410-659-9314

National Association for the Visually Handicapped

22 West 21st Street, New York, NY 10010
    212-889-3141

Nursing Homes

American Association of Homes and Services for the Aging

901 E Street, N.W., Suite 500, Washington, DC 20004
    202-783-2242
    http://www.senior.com/aahsa/aahsa-state.html

American Health Care Association

1201 L Street, N.W., Washington, DC 20005
    202-842-4444

Rehabilitation

American Occupational Therapy Association

4720 Montgomery Lane, Bethesda, MD 20814
   301-652-7590

American Physical Therapy Association

1111 North Fairfax Street, Alexandria, VA 22314
   800-999-APTA
   http://www.apta.org

American Rehabilitation Association

1910 Association Drive, Suite 200, Reston, VA 22091
   703-648-9300

Nursing Services

Visiting Nurse Associations of America

3801 East Florida, Suite 900, Denver, CO 80210
   800-426-2547
   You can also consult your phone book for the address and telephone
   number of the Visiting Nurse Association closest to you.

Volunteer and Employment Programs

National Senior Service Corps

1201 New York Avenue, N.W., Washington, DC 20525
   800-424-8867
   http://www.senior.com/npo/nssc.html
   Sponsors the Foster Grandparent Program, Retired and Senior
   Volunteer Program, and the Senior Companion Program.

Service Corps Of Retired Executives (SCORE)

409 Third Street, S.W., 4th Floor, Washington, DC 20024
   800-634-0245

American Association of Retired Persons (AARP)

601 E Street, N. W., Washington, DC 20049
   800-424-3410
   http://www.aarp.org/connect/html

Canadian Association of Retired Persons

27 Queen Street East, Suite 1304, Toronto, Ontario, Canada M5C 2M6
   416-363-8748
   http://www.thecareguide.com/CARP.html

Other Resources

National Asian Pacific Center on Aging

Suite 914, Melbourne Tower, 1511 3rd Avenue, Seattle, WA 98101
   206-624-1221

National Caucus and Center on Black Aged

1424 K Street, N.W., Suite 100, Washington, DC 20036
   202-637-8400

National Council on the Aging

409 Third Street, S.W., Suite 200, Washington, DC 20024
   202-479-1200
   http://www.shs.net/ncoa/ncoa.htm

National Hispanic Council on Aging
   2713 Ontario Road, N.W., Suite 200, Washington, DC 20009
   202-265-1288

Acknowledgments

Many thanks to

Benjamin H. Adler, Kenneth J. Doka, Eleanore Grater Lewis,
Susan Rosenburg, and Eileen Salmanson
who helped bring a measure of order out of chaos

our editor, Susan Worst,
who has given structure to our ideas with her valuable
suggestions, habitual carefulness, and attention to detail

and the countless aging parents and their children who have
shared their hearts and their minds.